Test your

Stress Resilience

**LIZ O'NEILL AND
BRIAN O'NEILL**

Series editors: GARETH LEWIS & GENE CROZIER

Hodder & Stoughton

A MEMBER OF THE HODDER HEADLINE GROUP

Dedicated to: Katie, Simon and Jamie from whom we have learned so much about stress.

Orders: please contact Bookpoint Ltd, 130 Milton Park, Abingdon, Oxon OX14 4SB.
Telephone: (44) 01235 400414, Fax: (44) 01235 400454. Lines are open from 9.00 – 6.00, Monday to Saturday, with a 24 hour message answering service.
Email address: orders@bookpoint.co.uk

British Library Cataloguing in Publication Data
A catalogue record for this title is available from The British Library

ISBN 0 340 802391

First published 2001
Impression number   10 9 8 7 6 5 4 3 2 1
Year   2004 2003 2002 2001

Copyright © 2001 Liz O'Neill and Brian O'Neill

All rights reserved. No part of this publication may re reproduced or transmitted in any form or by any means, electronic or mechanical, including photocopy, recording, or any information storage and retrieval system, without permission in writing from the publisher or under licence from the Copyright Licensing Agency Limited. Further details of such licences (for reprographic reproduction) may be obtained from the Copyright Licensing Agency Limited, 90 Tottenham Court Road, London W1P 9HE.

Typeset by Fakenham Photosetting Limited, Fakenham, Norfolk.
Printed in Great Britain for Hodder & Stoughton Education, a division of Hodder Headline Plc, 338 Euston Road, London NW1 3BH by Cox & Wyman Ltd, Reading, Berkshire.

in *the Institute of Management*

The Institute of Management (IM) is the leading organisation for professional management. Its purpose is to promote the art and science of management in every sector and at every level, through research, education, training and development, and representation of members' views on management issues.

This series is commissioned by IM Enterprises Limited, a subsidiary of the Institute of Management, providing commercial services.

**Management House,
Cottingham Road,
Corby,
Northants NN17 1TT
Tel: 01536 204222;
Fax: 01536 201651
Website: http://www.inst-mgt.org.uk**

Registered in England no 3834492
Registered office: 2 Savoy Court, Strand,
London WC2R 0EZ

Contents

Stress: An overview	5
Causes and effects of stress	18
Improving how you think	36
Healthy habits	52
Stress at work	69
Being resilient	85
Sources and references	95

Stress: An overview

Stress is no longer the mystery it once was. A great deal is known about its causes and how it can be resolved or managed. Our goal is to translate this knowledge into practical understanding and guidance. By working through the book you will learn:

- what stress means
- what causes it
- how stress affects your body, mind, emotions and behaviour
- how to recognise and respond to early signs
- how to respond to stressful events in your life
- what you can do to manage stress
- how to avoid and remove stressors in the workplace
- how to be resilient to pressure

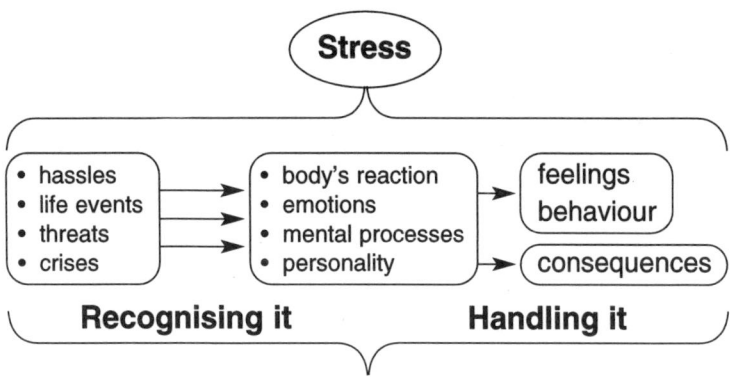

In this chapter we explore

- the great impact stress has
- the difficulty of recognising stress in ourselves
- the meaning of stress
- good and bad stress
- a framework for handling stress

But first, try our general knowledge quiz. Answers are at the end of the chapter.

Test yourself

The stress quiz

1. Which of the following countries has the unhappiest workers in the developed world?

    a. Britain

    b. Ireland

    c. France

    d. Holland

2. What percentage of staff turnover is believed to be caused by stress?

    a. 10%

    b. 25%

    c. 40%

    d. 60%

3. Which of the following is likely to be most stressful?

    a. sex difficulties

b. trouble with in-laws

c. retirement

d. being made redundant

4. Which of the following is the least effective way to handle stress?

   a. Think about how someone you respect would handle it and try that

   b. Put it to the back of your mind

   c. Look for a logical way to explain the situation

   d. Use your past experience

1. Stress is serious

Stress is acquiring a status as the killer of the 21st century. Witness these recent newspaper headlines:

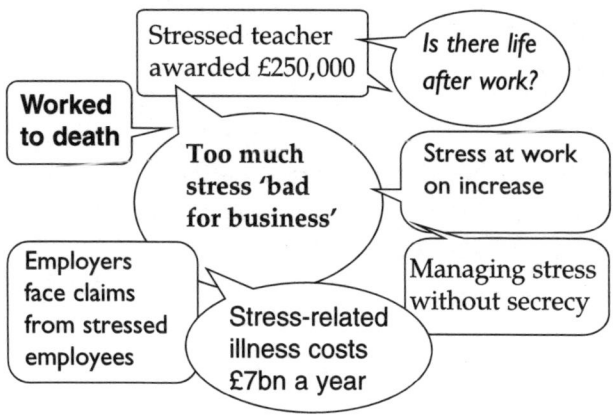

Stress is not new, of course. It has always been with us. What started to raise its profile among helping professionals was the effects it had on soldiers in World Wars I and II.

Large numbers of soldiers developed symptoms of stress ranging from mild anxiety to severe breakdowns and life-long handicap. Stress became known as shell-shock in WWI, battle fatigue in WWII and post-traumatic stress disorder after the Vietnam War; and the longer soldiers were exposed to battle conditions, the higher the incidence of severe stress.

Very few have experienced the trauma of war, but everyone has experience of the conditions of modern living that induce stress and emotional breakdown. Some of the major causes are easy to identify: job insecurity and unemployment, public transport and the trials of daily commuting, the toll of work on relationships, information overload, family arguments, the job, hostile bosses and customers, bullying and discrimination, poor service, too many demands and natural disasters such as flooding. In a recent survey, 44% of adults cited rush-hour traffic as the biggest cause of stress. Not hard to believe, is it?

> Curiously, although prosperity has risen and working conditions have improved, the levels of job satisfaction of British workers has actually *declined* over the last 25 years and stress is one of the major causes of this downward shift.
>
> *'Changes in UK work patterns have resulted in a 90% increase in mental and psychological claims over the past five years'*
>
> (UNUM, long-term disability insurers).

Stress exacts terrible costs in the workplace, no matter what kind of employer it is – businesses, public service organisations, educational institutions and charities. According to the Industrial Society, stress undermines performance and productivity in nine out of 10 organisations. It is estimated to cause half of the 360 million working days lost annually in the UK at a cost of £4 billion. And stressed employees are increasingly bringing successful legal action against their employers for work-induced stress.

It is not just stress at work. Every aspect of life is affected. Stress causes aches and pains and makes people vulnerable to illness. It makes life miserable. It reduces people's ability to function at work and it injures their relationships with others.

2. Recognising when you are stressed

If you ever feel stressed you are in good company. Most people experience some form of stress, many to a point where it disrupts their life. In the year 2000, 70% of working adults had experienced stress at work. American researchers have estimated that as many as 25 percent of the population are chronically stressed.

Are you stressed? This can be a surprisingly difficult question to answer, because it begs several further questions. What does it feel like to be stressed? What are the symptoms? Is what is going on in your life sufficient to cause stress? Isn't stress all in the mind anyway? Isn't it better to ignore it and just keep soldiering on? And, if you admit to being stressed doesn't that make you a weak person?

Crashing out

Times were unbelievably tough at the firm where Henry is supervisor. In serious difficulties, it was drastically cutting the workforce and introducing radical changes to its systems and work practices. Obliged to work a 70-hour week, Henry saw little of his family. He frequently felt wretched and knew that something was wrong. He had chronic headaches and difficulty concentrating and sleeping. He was on a short fuse. But it wasn't done to complain and Henry did not want to risk his job by taking time off, so he said nothing. What saved him, he says later, was coming down with pneumonia. Being ill gave him time to reflect, put things into proper order, and recharge his batteries. By the time he returned to work, he had made some hard decisions and brought his work life under control.

People do not always realise or admit when they are stressed. They soldier on as best they can, confused and not fully understanding what is going on. In their best selling book, *In Search of Excellence*, Tom Peters and Robert Waterman tell their boiled frog story to explain how this comes about. It goes like this:

If you were to catch a frog and pop it into a large pot of boiling water, it would immediately leap out because it would feel pain. Catch a second frog and pop it into a pot of cold water and it would swim about quite happily. Now suppose you gradually turned up the heat under the pot. What would this second frog do? The moral of the story is that the second frog, unaware that the temperature is gradually changing, would boil – slowly but inevitably.

Have you ever been a boiled frog? If the heat is turned up gradually you may not recognise you are stressed. You may not recognise stress if the pressure you feel is what you have come to accept as 'normal'. You may not recognise stress if the pressure brings a buzz of stimulation and excitement, or if it makes you feel important. Later we discuss the behavioural, physiological and mental signs for recognising stress.

3. Stress – what it means

While everyone has an intuitive understanding of stress, there is more to it than meets the eye. Stress is not simply anxiety, though anxiety is sometimes part of a stress reaction. Stress is not necessarily damaging. It is sometimes exciting as any avid football fan full knows. Overload or overstimulation is not the only cause of stress. Having too little to do and too little stimulation are sometimes stressful. Stress, finally, is not always something to avoid. It is a necessary part of life and high achievement.

> The Health & Safety Executive defines stress as:
>
> *'The reaction people have to excessive pressures or other types of demand placed on them. It arises when they worry that they can't cope.'*

A useful comparison is with a road bridge designed to carry heavy loads while resisting storms and earthquakes. Such forces put a strain on the structure of the bridge that the bridge will ordinarily withstand. But if the strain exceeds a certain point, it produces stresses that eventually destroy the bridge. People, similarly, are designed to cope with various environmental demands. But when the demands overload their physiological, psychological or social systems, they go over the edge. A person is said to be stressed when his or her resources are insufficient to cope with the demands coming from the environment.

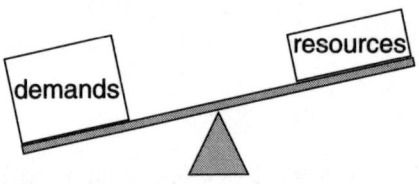

The answer to stress, therefore, seems obvious: reduce the demands; encourage people to work less; allow people flexible working hours; make life easier.

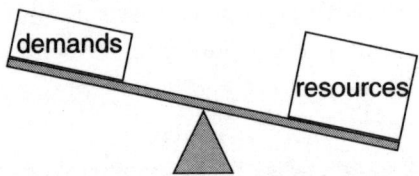

This solution is true but only to a point. While excessive pressure and demand cause stress, so can too little. Laboratory research has shown that no pressure of any kind leads to very poor performance and low well-being. Workers on a production line monitoring products for defects cannot sustain high performance for long. They become bored and dissatisfied. Similarly airport security personnel cannot keep monitoring the baggage x-ray

Stress: An overview

without breaks. People who are 'couch potatoes' are lethargic and their morale is lower than people who are active. A remarkable proportion of men who retire from active work at 65 do not live beyond the age of 68.

A certain amount of pressure is essential. The trick is to get the right balance between demands and resources.

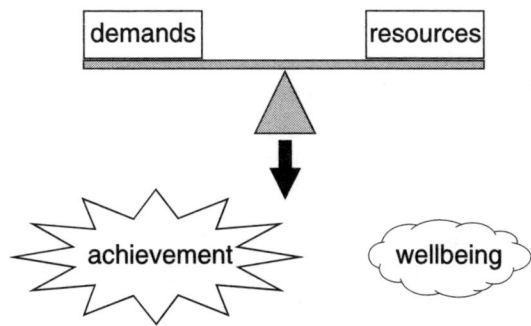

Test yourself

Your balance

Reviewing the three scales above, which one best describes your current situation?

☐ The demands I face are exceeding my resources

☐ The demands on me are insufficient – I need more challenge

☐ There is a good balance between the demands on me and my personal resources

Any initial thoughts about anything you want to improve?

4. Good stress and bad stress

So there is something positive about pressure. You need it to perform at your best, and that leads to good feelings about yourself. The stress curve below shows an optimum range of pressure where stress has this positive effect. Above and below that range is where stress is bad for you.

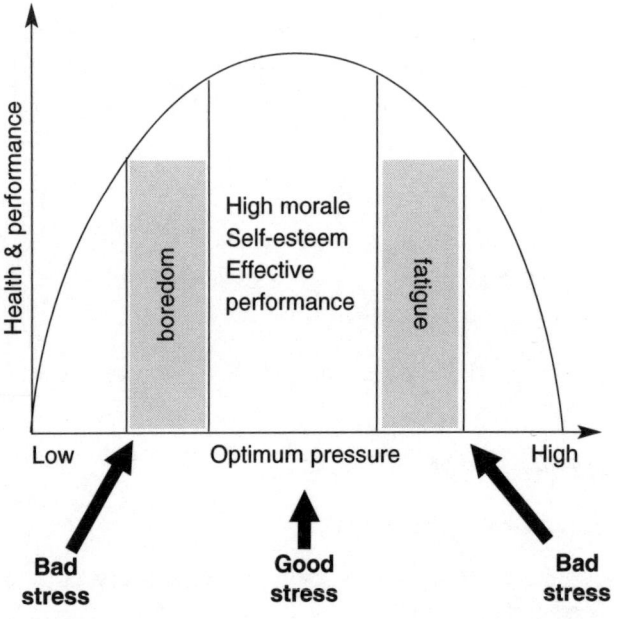

The stress curve

There is also a grey area between the optimum range and overstimulation. It is OK to push yourself into that grey area to achieve peak performance – running the 100 metres sprint or studying hard for an exam. But pushing too hard for too long stretches you beyond your limits, and that is what takes you into stress and eventual burnout.

Stress: An overview

Similarly, it may be comfortable 'veging out' occasionally when pressure falls below the optimum range. It is natural when the pressure comes off at the end of a project, an intensive training course or a strenuous season. However, very low levels of pressure for too long leads to feelings of intense boredom and sometimes depression. You switch off and become sleepy, sluggish and unmotivated.

One of the most interesting facts about stress is that everyone has a unique Stress Curve. Some people have a much higher tolerance for pressure, a much higher need for stimulation and challenge. Others, who have low stress tolerance, can cope with fewer demands.

> **Test yourself**
>
> **Your optimal stress level**
>
> With what level of pressure and challenge are you at your best?
>
> | *TV's Royle family* | | | | | *Steve Redgrave* |
> |---|---|---|---|---|---|
> | ☐ | ☐ | ☐ | ☐ | ☐ | ☐ |
>
> - very little pressure
> - jobs well within my reach
> - routine, recurring tasks
> - stability and continuity
>
> - lots of pressure and
> - challenges that stretch me beyond my limit
> - no two days the same
> - change and variety in life

> Steve Redgrave, the rower and BBC Sports Personality of the Year, has developed an unusual – perhaps unique – ability to cope with pressure. Consider the punishing schedule it took to win gold in five successive Olympics, and what this must have taken out of him physically and economically, as well as the costs to his family and social life.

We do not believe that the level of stress people can cope with is eternally fixed. By learning and practising sensible coping strategies, it should be possible to increase stress tolerance and improve one's quality of living.

4. A framework for handling stress

Broadly speaking, there are three areas in which stress may be handled effectively.

```
┌─────────────────────────────────────────────┐
│  1. The threats and demands you face        │
│  family, social, economic, work, physical,  │
│  other                                      │
└─────────────────────────────────────────────┘
                     ▼
┌─────────────────────────────────────────────┐
│  2. How you process the threats and demands │
│     physiology, health, personality,        │
│         mind-set, experience                │
└─────────────────────────────────────────────┘
                     ▼
┌─────────────────────────────────────────────┐
│ 3. How you respond to the threats and demands│
│  mind, control, emotional control, behaviour,│
│  strengthening your resistance, social support,│
│             work support                    │
└─────────────────────────────────────────────┘
```

Managing stress is about dealing with the demands directly – by eliminating, changing or avoiding them. It is about knowing yourself and your limits – and using this knowledge to interpret and handle the demands and threats. And it is about improving both your skills for responding and the support you require from others.

You will find facts and insights pertaining to these three areas throughout the book.

Chapter review

> Looking back over the chapter, are there any particular points you will take from it?

Answers to the quiz
1. a. Britain. International research by Andrew Oswald and David Blanchflower has shown that only Japanese and Hungarian workers report lower levels of unhappiness.
2. c. Stress is believed to cause a whopping 40% of staff turnover.
3. d. Being fired or made redundant requires a huge amount of adjustment (Miller and Rahe, 1997).
4. b. By putting stress to the back of your mind you risk having it come to trouble you.

Causes and effects of stress

In this chapter we explore:

- the threats and demands that cause stress
- how the body reacts to stress
- the role of the mind and personality factors in stress
- how to recognise when you are stressed

1. Threats and demands

There is no shortage of stressors in everyday life. Even positive events such as marriage, birth of a child, moving to a better house or a promotion can be stressful. Some stressors, such as moving house, happen only once or very infrequently. Others – commuting, a troubled relationship – are more continuous and enduring.

Stress is cumulative. The higher the total score, the more serious is the stress reaction. You may cope well with the adjustments required when you change job. But moving house as well, settling the children into new schools, and spending Christmas with the extended family may bring too much stress to cope with. That is often why people overreact to something trivial. The last straw in a whole batch of hassles, it might be enough to trigger the emotional storm.

Going over the top

After a meteoric rise, Sarah has been promoted to the board of Delphic Advertising. At 33 she is the youngest director. She finds her job intensely fulfilling despite an ever-increasing workload. This morning, tired after a late dinner with clients, she is in no mood to discuss their wedding plans with David, her partner. In fact, she has not been sleeping well. Now, squeezed between fellow-passengers on the commuter train, the last thing she feels is fulfilled. Leaves on the line are causing a 45-minute delay. Arriving breathless at the office she learns that the client she was to meet would not wait. Minutes later, as her best copywriter is telling her she is pregnant, the managing director storms into her office. He wants to know just what the hell she means standing up such an important client. With voice shaking and stomach churning, Sarah tries to explain but he has none of it.

Later, Sarah is working on an important presentation. She finds it difficult to concentrate and her thoughts drift to David ... they seldom see each other and only argue when they do. These days, sex is the last thing on her mind and she can't make up her mind about the wedding date. With her career consuming so much of her life, she cannot remember when she last saw her girl friends.

Leaving the office at 7:30 is now a habit. Again the train is delayed and she gets home late, emotionally drained and exhausted. As she pours herself a stiff drink, David comes in and says 'Where have you been?'. That's when Sarah loses it. Hurling the glass at his head, she screams, 'How dare you criticise me like that!', then bursts into tears.

> **? Test yourself**
>
> **Coping with stress**
>
> Imagine you are David and you don't know what kind of day Sarah has had. How would you respond to her outburst?
>
> a. Quietly clear up the mess, leave the room and give her time to regain composure.
>
> b. Give her a hug and say, 'I wasn't criticising you, silly. Now what would you like for supper?'
>
> c. Say to her: 'You must be feeling awful, Sarah. Do you want to talk about it?'
>
> d. Say to her: 'The hours you are working are doing neither of us any good. You've got to slow down'.
>
> Answer at the end of the chapter.

When struggling to cope with strong emotion, it is difficult to act or speak rationally. At the point when Sarah sees red, she is incapable of talking sensibly or making sensible decisions. By showing empathy David will encourage her to vent her feelings. By encouraging her to talk he will help her to explain why she is upset. And if he listens attentively, he enables her to address the underlying conflict. It takes time, patience and understanding to move from the emotional storm to a sensible discussion of the issues.

Do an audit of the events that brought Sarah to the blow-up with David. Distinguish between stressors that are one-off and have a short life and stressors that endure over time. Distinguish also between stressors that are seriously stressful and stressors that are relatively innocuous. And think of the crossover effects of one stressor on another. In

Sarah's case, work-based stressors are crossing over to increase the tension in her relationship with David. Suggested answers can be found at the end of the chapter.

Here is a catalogue of the most common stressors.

Common stressors	*Examples*	
• Disasters and crises	Business collapse, flooding and other natural disasters, major accident, serious crime	☐
• Life events	Moving house, marriage, divorce, pregnancy, ageing, retirement, a large mortgage, Christmas	☐
• Other family factors	Death in family, marital and parent-child conflicts, illness, children leaving home	☐
• Work factors	Sick building syndrome, trouble with boss, overwork, routine, role conflict, ambiguity, being fired	☐
• Change	School, relationships, work, responsibilities, finances	☐
• Everyday hassles	Travel, being late, noise, losing something, arguments, rudeness	☐
• Expectations	To work late, to turn the other cheek, to comply under duress	☐
• Cultural conflicts	Pressure to conform to a sub-culture in a multi-cultural society	☐

Some stressful events are more difficult and take longer to adjust to than others. In research studies, groups from the general population have rated the amount of adjustment that various stressors required. The following scores summarise these adjustment ratings:

Life event	Score
Divorce	98
Losing your job	79
Pregnancy	66
Change in financial status	56
Change to different work	51
Substantial mortgage or debt	44
Marriage	50
Trouble with in-laws	38
Great personal achievement	37
Christmas	30
Trouble with boss	29
Holiday	25

(Based on Miller and Rahe, 1997)

Causes and effects of stress

Quite obviously, the more you know about the things that are causing you stress, the more you can do about them. So take time to complete the next exercise.

? Test yourself

Stress events audit

From the Common Stressor and Life Events identify which, if any, are causing you stress right now. Note your stressors in the appropriate quadrant below.

	One-off	Enduring
Very stressful		
Somewhat stressful		

- Which of the stressors would you like to tackle most?
- How have you dealt with that stress or until now?
- Are there any crossover stressors in your audit?

How the body reacts to stress

People have recognisable reactions to threats, demands and hassles. Sarah, for instance, is experiencing some of the most familiar stress reactions:

- sleep difficulty
- voice tremor
- stomach upset
- feeling unfulfilled
- difficulty concentrating
- loss of social contact
- loss of sexual interest
- feeling emotionally drained
- use of alcohol for relaxation
- low self-control
- over-sensitivity

Because the physiology of the body is programmed to react to stress in these ways, her reactions are predictable and understandable. This next case study develops this idea.

> Imagine you are driving on the motorway, your thoughts on the important meeting that lies ahead. It is dark, raining and visibility is poor. As an exit approaches, a car from the outside lane suddenly swerves right across your path, missing your car by a hair's breadth. How do you react?

Hopefully, your feet and hands will react automatically to slow and bring your vehicle safely under control. And very possibly your voice will rise in pitch as you curse the delinquent driver. Here are some other probable reactions and their short-term advantages for your survival:

Reactions

- eyes wide, pupils dilated
- increased heart and blood pressure
- improved blood supply to the brain
- serious mood
- quickened breathing
- stomach churns
- increased sweat

Advantages

- you see more
- increased blood sugar and oxygen supply
- more alert, clearer thinking
- better concentration
- increases oxygen to muscles and cools body
- blood channelled to where it is needed most
- cools the body

In emergencies and crises, the brain centre responsible for self-control, judgement and decision-making is no longer fully in command. We noted that in Sarah's case. It is the more primitive mid-brain and the autonomic nervous system that rule. They pump adrenaline into the bloodstream and produce the above reactions. They are programmed to mobilise the body's systems for fight or flight, and to redistribute the body's resources to cope with the threat. The reactions listed above are part of the fight or flight pattern.

The fight or flight mechanism works brilliantly in an emergency to deal with threat. Normally, this is followed by a period of relief and recovery and return to stability. So, if you continued your journey on the motorway your body would gradually return to its normal levels. It is programmed to maintain a 'steady state'. If, however, emergency responses are triggered too frequently, the body is never able to 'gear down' from its state of super-alertness. Damage can eventually result, such as:

- chronic tension headaches and migraine
- chest pains
- blood pressure problems
- muscle aches
- anxiety, no sense of humour
- irritable bowel syndrome
- indigestion and ulcers
- itching and rashes

There is medical evidence that prolonged stress has the effect of depleting the immunological system. This in turn can lead to illness, such as colds and 'flu, and slow the healing of wounds. Stress is also associated with life-threatening illnesses such as cardiac disease and cancer.

But these effects depend on the individual and his or her unique physical make-up. One of the authors reacts instantly to stress with indigestion and an upset stomach. The other has crippling muscle spasms in her back. These individual vulnerabilities appear to be handed down genetically.

Other behavioural reactions to stress
Stress is known to cause alcohol abuse, smoking, appetite disorder, social withdrawal, accident-proneness and domestic violence.

2. The role of the mind and personality

Stress is caused by how you *appraise* an event, not by the event itself. The event will be stressful or not depending on its meaning and importance *for the individual*. Examples:

- Employees react differently when their company is being sold. One, interpreting the take-over as a threat to job security, is stressed. Another sees it as an exciting opportunity for career advancement, while a third, who sees her job as temporary, is indifferent.
- Taking an examination is stressful for one student, but a challenge and opportunity for another.
- An open-plan office is irritating for some but an opportunity to socialise for others.

Let's play out more of the motorway incident to see what is happening here.

> Braking, you manage to bring your car to a skidding halt on the hard shoulder. When you resume the journey, fear turns to incandescent anger. As you approach your destination your memory keeps replaying the incident. You keep reliving the original shock, fear and anger. Arriving at the meeting place you are in total emotional turmoil. You can't think straight and the important meeting is a disaster.

Other people would react differently to the situation – with relief, with exasperation, with a protracted burn (as above) or with all-out road rage. That is because individuals respond differently to stress at the psychological as well as the physical level. When appraising an event, their *perceptions*, *beliefs*, and *personality* come into play at an incredibly fast speed. We describe below characteristics that greatly affect how people react to and cope with stress.

Drivers

Clinical experts have identified five ingrained beliefs or *drivers* which everyone shows some of the time. Most people favour one in particular. The drivers are sources of stress for some people. Operating like an internal tape, the driver continually repeats the same compulsive messages over and over. You may recognise yours in this list.

Driver	The meaning and the consequences
Be Perfect	Having impossibly high standards – never satisfied with what you do, you exceed what is practical.
Please Others	Always doing what others ask – not what you want, often to your disadvantage.
Hurry Up	Always rushing about – 'busy fool', leaving things until too late.
Try Harder	Striving, what counts is the effort not the result – lack of focus, persevering too far.
Be Strong	Always shouldering the burden without complaint – others turn to you for help, but no one comforts you.

Drivers lead to compulsive behaviours, not to free choices. Striving always to satisfy the drivers brings tension and stress. A large Please Others driver might lead you to believe that you were somehow at fault in the motorway incident. A Be Strong driver might lead you to bottle up the incident and create more tension for yourself.

Type A personality

Type A personality types are hard driving, conscientious workaholics. Very competitive, impatient and aggressive, they operate on a short fuse. They are continually driven to achieve more in less time. Their behaviour is compulsive and they have little time for introspection. The Type B personality is quite different – measured, less harried, and less competitive though just as ambitious and intelligent. In our motorway incident, the Type A response is likely to be aggressive and the Type B to be more measured. Do you see yourself as either of these types?

The links between Type A behaviour pattern and stress are well documented. Type A individuals are inclined to interpret neutral situations as threatening and stressful. They report higher levels of stress and tension than Type Bs. And Type A behaviour, particularly the hostile component, appears to contribute to coronary heart disease.

Locus of control (LOC)

Another characteristic that is widely studied in stress is *locus of control*. People with an *external* LOC believe that events are controlled by luck and fate. Things happen regardless of what they might do to control them. They are helpless. Individuals who have an *internal* LOC believe the opposite. They believe that their decisions and actions make a genuine difference.

In the motorway incident, the high LOC driver would regain self-control more quickly and be composed for the meeting.

Test yourself

Locus of control

This exercise is not a rigorous test and is meant only to stimulate your thinking. Circle the numbers showing how strongly you agree or disagree with each statement. Ticks on the left always mean 'disagree'. Ticks to the right always mean 'agree'.

	Disagree				*Agree*
1. Getting ahead is about what you can do not who you know.	1	2	3	4	5
2. I am too old to change.	5	4	3	2	1
3. A good way to handle a problem is not to think about it.	5	4	3	2	1
4. Promotions are earned through hard work and persistence.	1	2	3	4	5
5. I am very persevering – and I usually accomplish what I set out to do.	1	2	3	4	5
6. Because no one can predict the future there's little point in making plans.	5	4	3	2	1
7. I won't make resolutions because I don't usually keep them.	5	4	3	2	1
8. I believe we are masters of our own fate.	1	2	3	4	5

> A score of 32 suggests you feel in control of your life and what happens to you, good and bad. You are likely to take initiative in handling stress and its causes. A score of 24 to 31 also suggests internal control, though less definitely.
>
> A score of 8 or lower suggests the opposite – a feeling you don't have much control over what happens. A score of 9 to 19 is in the same direction. Perhaps you could be taking more control of the events that are stressing you.

Self-efficacy and optimism

These personality traits are rather similar in effect to LOC. High self-efficacy is a belief in one's ability to master all kinds of challenges. It is a conviction you can do whatever it takes to achieve your goal. Optimism is a general expectation that good things will happen as opposed to pessimism, an assumption that the worst will happen. In our motorway case, the effect of self-efficacy and optimism would be similar to internal LOC.

All three characteristics are personal resources against stress. People with internal LOC, high self-efficacy and general optimism tend to think and act differently from those who have the opposite traits. First they interpret and evaluate situations more realistically and positively. They can see opportunities or silver linings not just threats and dark clouds. Second, they are more proactive and positive in their coping strategies. And third, their personality acts as a protective buffer against the effects of stress on ill health.

Differences in individuals make-up means that there are striking differences in how they respond to stress. Once stress is triggered, however, common reactions are aroused as the next section shows.

3. How to recognise when you are stressed

To avoid the fate of the boiled frog you need to pay attention to your reactions whenever demands and threats increase. There are physiological, behavioural, emotional, mental and interpersonal reactions to monitor. Any one of these might be in itself unimportant. But when it is one among several, and they are disturbing your life, then you need to remove yourself smartly from the boiling water.

Test yourself

Stress reactions audit

Here is an exercise to help you monitor your stress reactions. Every day, make three of four periodic spot checks of your feelings and behaviour. If you observe any of the reactions listed below, make a note in your diary. Note also the severity of the reaction: A = mild, B = unpleasant, C = seriously disruptive. This record of stress reactions will provide an informed basis upon which to judge your stress level. At the end of each week, review your entries and form a view of your stress level.

The list may also be used as a questionnaire to audit the stress levels of a team or a department. Invite those who are involved to:

- tick the first column if they have recently observed the sign in themselves more than once or twice

- tick the second column if they have personal concerns about the signs they have ticked

- add the number of ticks in the second column to get a sense of the size of the problem

Causes and effects of stress

	✔	☹

1. Headaches, faint or dizzy
2. Trouble getting my breath
3. Nervous or shaky inside
4. Pain in heart or chest, heart pounding
5. Sore muscles or pains in lower back
6. Itching, sweating or trembling
7. Constipation or loose bowels
8. Hot or cold spells
9. Poor appetite, nausea, upset stomach
10. Weak or heavy feelings in part of body
11. Low in energy or slowed down
12. Difficulty falling asleep or staying asleep
13. Loss of sexual interest or pleasure
14. Use alcohol regularly to de-stress
15. Heavy smoking
16. No interest in things
17. Feel blocked, unable to get things done
18. Worry, stew about things, feel trapped
19. Tense or keyed up, crying easily
20. Hopeless about the future, depressed
21. Afraid for no obvious reason
22. Difficulty making decisions

Test Your Stress Resilience

	✔	☹
23. Have to check/double check what I do		
24. Worried about sloppiness/carelessness		
25. Have to do things slowly to be sure I do them right		
26. Trouble concentrating		
27. Trouble remembering things, forgetful		
28. Bad dreams or bad thoughts		
29. Others unsympathetic don't understand me		
30. Unusually critical of others, making enemies		
31. Lonely or want to be alone		
32. Disagreements and arguments with friends and family		
33. Feel people are unfriendly or dislike me		

- How would you rate your overall stress level at this time?
- Would your partner or best friend agree with your assessment?
- What do you think is causing the stress?

Chapter review

> Looking back over the chapter, are there any particular points you will take from it?

Causes and effects of stress

Test Yourself answers
1. The preferred response from David is option c.
2. The probable stressors leading up to Sarah's outburst:

Non-work
- outstanding personal achievement
- increased income
- impending marriage
- arguments with partner
- change in social activities

Work
- workload
- commuting
- change in responsibilities
- trouble with boss
- change in work hours

Improving how you think

In this chapter we consider the following well-tested tactics for challenging negative thinking and shifting into constructive thinking:

- recognise when your thinking is pessimistic and getting in the way
- asking challenging questions
- talking to yourself positively
- giving yourself choices
- controlling your attention
- keeping a thought diary

Using these tactics will make you feel less anxious and better able to cope with pressures and difficulties.

Philosophers through the ages have reasoned that

'men [and women] are disturbed not by things, but by the view they take of them' (Epectitus).

It's not what you see, or what happens that makes the difference to how you feel or what you do. It is how you *interpret* it.

This simple framework developed by the renowned psychologist, Albert Ellis, helps us understand how thinking affects stress:

Improving how you think

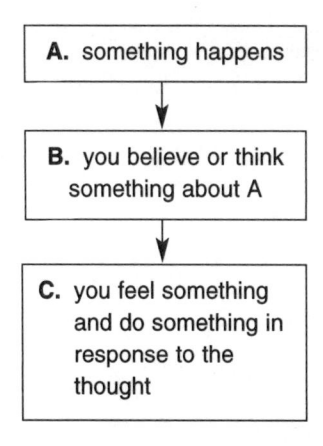

```
A. something happens
        ↓
B. you believe or think
   something about A
        ↓
C. you feel something
   and do something in
   response to the
   thought
```

Most of the time you are only aware of what happens at points A and C. But what happens is a result of what you were thinking at point B. Thinking about what's going on in your head (B) can help you better manage yourself and the demands you face. 'Stinking thinking' is rigid, illogical, self-defeating and a cause of stress. And realistic, logical and positive thinking can be immensely helpful in managing stress.

If you want to change how you *feel* you need to change how you *think*. First, it helps to have a real context within which to change your thinking. So think of a real time and place in which you felt seriously pressured. Things were getting on top of you. Perhaps your sleep was disturbed or you felt aches and pains. Maybe you were not getting on well with a person or persons in your family or at work. You were feeling tense and anxious. You felt stretched beyond your limit and close to the end of your tether. Can you recall such an event or period in your life?

> **? Test yourself**
>
> **A personal case**
>
> Make a note of the actual situation in just a few words.
>
> When did it happen?
>
> Name anyone who was involved in the situation
>
> ... and how they were involved
>
> Describe the kind of thoughts you were having at the time
>
> ... and the feelings you experienced
>
> Keep referring to this personal case when you read about the constructive-thinking tactics.

1. Recognising stinking thinking

Unless you are one of those rare people who are blessed with a sunny good nature, there will be days when everything looks black – or a dirty shade of grey at best. You wish you could go back to bed and start all over again – and so do your family and colleagues! Under prolonged pressure this kind of negative thinking often becomes more than a one-day wonder. It becomes a habit and you can get locked into stinking thinking about the world without realising it. So, when you are faced with a problem, the negative ways of thinking colour how you see the situation. And this, in turn, affects how you feel and what you do about it.

You need to catch yourself on the downward slopes. Surprisingly, people often don't notice it happening to them until they hit the bottom. We mentioned earlier these obvious clues to watch out for:

- Feeling anxious and pressured and your tension is rising.
- Feeling unremittingly low in spirits.
- Your views are consistently gloomier than those around you. Their clouds have silver linings but yours are uniformly black.
- Looking for excuses to have a good rant.
- Having a shorter fuse than before.
- Finding it difficult to concentrate or remember things.
- Worrying unrealistically.

These are sure signs that you need to stop and examine your thinking. When you recognise the signs, stop and ask yourself: what's going through my mind right now? What am I saying to myself?

We have already considered the negative drivers that can influence thinking and behaviour. Although they may appear to be positive motivators, these implicit drivers are compulsive and counter-productive. They do not motivate people to healthy achievement but bring tension and stress.

Driving yourself to 'be perfect', for example, means being constantly haunted by 'shoulds' and 'musts' but never quite living up to impossible unconscious standards. If you are constantly driven to 'please others' you rarely if ever do anything to please yourself. You get caught up in a cycle of worried thoughts and increasing anxiety.

The importance of what goes on in your head to how you feel and what you do was recognised in sports with the publication of books like *The Inner Game of Tennis*.

'Inner' meant the player's internal state. What the author Gallwey called 'the opponent within one's head [that was] more formidable than the one on the other side of the net'. Winning and success meant first defeating that *internal* opponent.

When it comes to stress you sometimes have to defeat that internal opponent within your head. That opponent makes *negative self talk* which means talking yourself down into a state of defeat and despair. When your self talk is negative or restricting or is making you feel lousy it can contribute to how stressed you feel and how you act. So it is essential to recognise when you are doing it.

Test yourself

Recognising the signs

Have you caught yourself doing yourself down in any of these ways? Give a double tick to the one you use a lot.

All-or-nothing thinking	'once a failure, always a failure'	☐
Catastrophising	'If I don't get this job I'll never work again' – anticipating total disaster	☐
Musterbating	'I must get it right first time or I'm a terrible person' – 'Be Perfect' in overdrive	☐
Over-generalising	'I messed this up – I'll never amount to anything' – everything is awful because of one bad experience	☐

Improving how you think

Jumping to conclusions	'He didn't look at me. I must have offended him'	☐
Emotional reasoning	'I feel guilty so I must have done something bad' – using feeling as evidence	☐
Personalising	'My boss looks cross this morning. I bet it was something I did'	☐

2. Asking yourself challenging questions

By challenging your negative thinking you weaken its impact. With continued practice this interrupts the downward spiral.

Test yourself

A personal case study

Think back to your personal case above. Imagine it is happening right now. Challenge your thinking with these questions. Might they help clarify your thinking in future? Tick the questions you think you can use.

Challenges	*Benefits*	
'Are there reasons for my having this worrying thought?'	This helps to work out where the worry is coming from.	☐
'Are there reasons against my holding this thought?'	You look for other, more positive, ways of seeing the situation.	☐
'What is the worst thing that could happen?'	This puts things in a realistic perspective – maybe the worst is not so very bad.	☐

'What are the chances of this happening?'	This helps you evaluate the risks realistically.	☐
'How could I cope with this?'	This calls up how you have coped before, the skills and assets you can bring to bear to the current situation.	☐
'What is a more constructive way of thinking about this?'	You formulate more rational and manageable ways of thinking about your worry.	☐

The questioning sounds dead simple, and it is. But of course it isn't as easy when you are in a slump. So it takes practice. When the questioning becomes a habit, of course, you use them all the time.

3. Talking to yourself positively

Talking to yourself sounds eccentric and hardly the advice you would expect from a professional. In fact, people mentally talk to themselves most of the time. Making a running commentary on what is going on, what one thinks about it, and how one interprets it is all part of the ongoing process of making sense of the world.

> It is incredibly difficult to avoid self talk. Close your eyes for 30 seconds and think of nothing..................
>
> It's just not possible to stop the inner dialogue is it?

Improving how you think

As we noted above, self-talking can be negative and pessimistic, and the negative words we say to ourselves stimulate negative thought and feelings, which lead to negative actions.

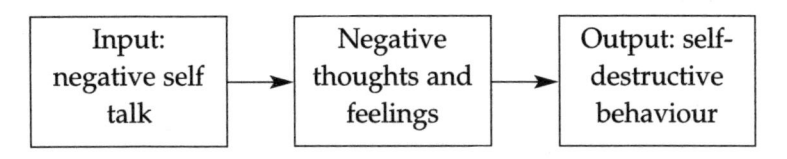

Input: negative self talk	→	Negative thoughts and feelings	→	Output: self-destructive behaviour

Conversely, by putting in something positive you will be more likely to have a positive output. That is, through positive self talk you can feel differently and act differently.

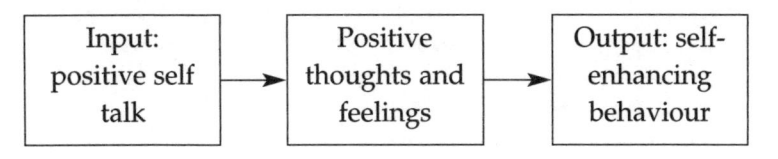

Input: positive self talk	→	Positive thoughts and feelings	→	Output: self-enhancing behaviour

So whenever you catch yourself in destructive self-talk, switch immediately to the constructive kind. Recall the things you have achieved that make you proud. Replay your positive qualities and strengths. Talk about the desirable happenings and the positive outcomes that you can anticipate. Think of your glass as half full not half empty.

? Test yourself

Applying positive self-talk

Self-talk can help you stay calm and reduce tension before, during and after a stressful situation. Review these self-talk suggestions. Ask yourself: 'If I had tried this would it have helped in the situation I described in my case study?'

Before
Tell yourself to stay calm. Say, 'Relax. Take it easy. Take a deep breath.'
Focus on your preparation. Say to yourself
'What do I have to do?
What's my plan?
It may be rough but I can handle this.
I won't take this personally.'

During
Reassure yourself that you can handle it. Say to yourself,
'I can meet this challenge
Relax – I'm in control
I'll deal with this stage by stage – one point at a time.'

After
Look back and see what you've learned. Say to yourself,
'I handled it pretty well.
It wasn't as bad as I expected.
Each time I do it it gets easier.
It didn't work that time – OK – what did I learn?'

4. Giving yourself choices

Being stressed is often associated with feeling trapped. Think carefully about this statement: 'I must give up smoking'. Or this one: 'I must lose weight.' What feelings do these statements arouse in you? Statements like 'I ought to' and 'I must not' imply compulsion and an absence of choice. Now consider these statements: 'I choose to give up smoking' and 'I choose to eat differently'. How does that feel? Managing stress is about recognising and giving yourself choices. You can tell yourself, 'I choose to' or 'I choose not to'. By choosing you affirm that you are an active agent in your life rather than as someone always reacting to demands.

There is *always* choice, even if some of the options seem at first sight to be difficult or unacceptable. And there are always consequences of choices. Using a questioning method like the one described earlier can help you think about the consequences of the various options in a constructive way.

> ### Regaining control
>
> Questions you might ask yourself next time you find yourself saying 'I ought to' or 'I must'
>
> - 'What do I choose to do?'
> - 'What will be the consequences of doing this?'
> - 'How can I manage these consequences?'
> - 'What other choices do I have?'
> - 'What will be the consequences of choosing to do something else?'
> - 'How can I manage these consequences?'

Choice also means taking responsible risks. When stressed and feeling down, it can be difficult to entertain possibilities that may not work out. The tendency is to play it safe and avoid risk. The effect, of course, is never to do anything different or exciting. And to close down opportunities for greater prosperity and satisfaction. Rather than dismiss possibilities out of hand, think instead about how you might manage the consequences. Managing the consequences may be less stressful than you imagined. It also means that sometimes you can 'think the unthinkable' and find out that it is not so unthinkable after all.

5. Controlling your attention

Often the problem is not a stressful event itself but our recalling it time after time. We keep replaying the memory and the unpleasant feelings associated with that memory. The memories return, control our attention and prevent us from focusing on the concerns of the present.

> Think back to the motorway incident on page 27. You may recall that John's sales presentation was a total disaster. Not because he had been cut up, but because he has kept replaying the motorway experience in his memory, and that took his eye right off the ball. It may have happened to you. You become locked in to something that happened yesterday or months ago, and that memory can completely cloud your thinking.
>
> Anyone who has been at the centre of a stressful change at work will recognise the signs. Initially people may have feelings of insecurity and anxiety, perhaps anger. But soon they come around to accepting the new ways and look positively to the future. But some people do not adapt well to change. They find it difficult to let go of past injuries, real and imagined. They can often be heard replaying the past. This clouded thinking makes it impossible for them to focus on the present, and they get left, literally, behind.

The University of York Work Skills Centre have developed very practical ways to get out of this downward spiral. Think of a house with two doors. A flood is pressing against the front door. The house is like your mind, and the flood is all the memories and emotions that are clamouring for your attention. You can try to cope with this pressure in various ways. You might try to cope by replaying the worrying situation in your mind, going over again what happened and what you did, worrying away at it. This does not work and you drown in the flood. Denial works by piling all the furniture up against the door and hoping it will all go away. But that does not work for long either. At some point the pressure bursts the door open and you drown in the flood.

If you want to control the stress, it means first recognising that the flood will not go away. Don't pretend it's not there. Next, recognise that the house has a loft into which you can go while the flood passes underneath. This is equivalent to stepping back from the stress event, deliberately placing your emotional memories on hold, and looking at it rationally for what it is. Think about the situation as if it were someone else, not you, involved in it. Put some distance between you and it.

Now pay attention to the tensions in your body. Stop and check out how your body is reacting. You will probably find that you are braced for action. Your shoulders are raised. Your face is frowning. You are sitting on the edge of your seat. Very deliberately allow the tension to go from your shoulders, your neck, your whole body. Relax your face muscles.

The next step is to rethink how you see the situation:

Rethinking the situation

- Think about how someone you respect would handle it and try that
- Look for a logical way to explain the situation
- Use your past experience

- Take one step at a time
- Find out more before you make a decision
- See it as a challenge that must be met
- Separate yourself from the problem and see it as something 'out there' that you are capable of dealing with

Finally, accept that the situation happened and choose to leave it behind you. Move on.

Wei-chi the Chinese word for crisis has two meanings: danger and opportunity. Stressful situations can have both meanings too: danger if you try to hold back the flood; and opportunity if you go into the attic, letting it flow by you and learning new ways of coping.

6. Keeping a thought diary

Another stress-management technique is to keep a *thought diary*. Every day for a week, monitor your stress levels and the events that cause them. Note when you feel particularly worried, frightened or anxious. It is easy to forget the details. So write them down as close to the time of the event as possible. Here is an outline to follow.

Thought diary

Date/time:

- Describe the thoughts going through your mind.
- What feelings do you have when you think those thoughts?

> - Rate how intense the feelings are on a scale from 1–10.
>
> *Normal*   *Maximum*
> *intensity*   *intensity*
>
> 1   2   3   4   5   6   7   8   9   10
>
> - Analyse your thoughts for evidence of stinking thinking.
> - Challenge this thinking vigorously.
> - Re-evaluate your feelings about the situation now on the scale.

Keeping a thought diary is a bit like dieting. It is difficult to do at first and the benefits do not kick in immediately. You will have good days and bad days. But with time you become practised at asking yourself the questions and challenging the worrying thoughts, and eventually you win control over stress.

7. Thoughts to live by

For many the written word is a deep and comforting well to draw from in times of trouble. Sometimes it takes the form of prayer. At others, it is a consoling thought remembered. Do you have any such thoughts to restore peace of mind when things are black? Here are our favourites.

> 'Give me the courage to change the things that can be changed, the fortitude to accept those which can't be changed and the wisdom to tell the difference between the two.'

Pick More Daisies

If I had to live my life over again, I'd dare to make more mistakes next time.
I'd relax.
I would limber up.
I would be sillier than I have been this trip.
I would take fewer things seriously.
I would take more chances.
I would take more trips.
I would climb more mountains, swim more rivers.
I would eat more ice cream and less beans.
I would perhaps have more actual troubles but I'd have fewer imaginary ones.
You see I'm one of those people who live seriously and
sanely hour after hour, day after day.
Oh, I've had my moments. And if I had to do it over again,
I'd have more of them.
In fact I'd try to have nothing else, just moments, one after
another, instead of living so many years ahead of each day.
I've been one of those persons who never goes anywhere
without a thermometer, a hot water bottle, a raincoat and
a parachute.
If I had to do it over again, I would travel lighter than I have.

> If I had to live my life over. I would start barefoot earlier
> in the spring and stay that way later in the fall.
> I would go to more dances.
> I would ride more merry-go-rounds.
> I would pick more daisies.
> *Nadine Stair, age 85*

Chapter review: what you will think differently

> What three thoughts will you take away from this chapter?

Healthy habits

Chapter 3 was about improving how you *think* about stressful situations. This chapter is about what you can *do* to help avoid stress and manage it successfully. You can exercise greater control over the pressures and hassles by:

- organising your time effectively
- asserting yourself
- looking after yourself
- maintaining effective relationships and networks

1. Managing time to avoid stress

Time pressures and deadlines were top sources of stress reported by managers in an Institute of Management survey. In fact, time pressure is probably the most common source of stress for most people. You become caught in a chronic time trap where there are not enough hours in the day. You run out of week before you run out of things to do.

Monitoring where the time goes
The first step is to find out exactly how you spend your time. Is it how you *think* you spend it? And is it how you *want* to spend it?

Monitoring your time

- Keep a diary for a week or so to find out how you are spending your time.
- At the end of the week review where your time is being spent.

> - Is the balance about right between time spent on meeting work demands and on meeting home demands?
> - And between time spent on meeting external demands and on meeting your own needs?
> - Are there any changes you'd like to make in this balance?

No matter how hard you try you will not find more hours in the day. What you *can* do is to manage the time there is better.

Managing your priorities
Setting priorities is about deciding what the really important things are and then making sure you stick to them.

> ### Knowing your priorities
>
> Imagine your are standing on a street corner on a windy day. You are clutching a handful of notes – 95 are £5 and 3 are £100 notes. The wind blows them out of your hands. Which of the notes do you chase? Do you know what your £100 priorities are? Are you putting time into achieving them?

Pareto, a nineteenth century Italian economist, was author of what became known as the Pareto Principle or 80/20 rule. This is a simple but incredibly useful rule of thumb for focusing one's energies. Concentrate your efforts on the 20% of your activities that deliver 80% of the important results.

We are often tempted to concentrate on activities that are easy and interesting and that we can comfortably do. But frequently these are low-priority activities that have a limited pay-off. So keep checking if you are you putting 80% of your time and effort into the £100 priorities.

Sometimes because of pressure you find yourself simply doing what is urgent. The risk is that you neglect what is important. And these are what may save you time and support the attainment of long-term goals. You might, for example, be thinking, 'I must get this done' when your thought should be, 'I must train my staff'. You might think, 'I must improve my PC skills' rather than, 'It's quicker if I write this in long hand.'

Notice that urgent and important are not different criteria for setting priorities. Combining the two gives the following decision-making matrix. Clearly pressures that are both important and urgent should receive one's fullest attention, and, of course, those that are neither should immediately be dropped.

Urgent	Low — Important — High
High	**Fire-fighting** — If it isn't important why is it urgent? Do you need to do more planning? Or re-negotiate arbitary deadlines? / **Red hot priorities** — These activities give the high 80% pay-off. They deserve your quality time and attention. Do them now!
Low	**Drop them** — These are not going to make much difference and no one is shouting for them. / **Hot priorities** — No time pressure, but these activities will make a difference. Do them!

Healthy habits

❓ Test Yourself

Getting the priorities right at work

- Consider the areas in your working life which take up time and energy, and are potential sources of stress

- Now think carefully ... are you devoting your energies to the right priorities?

- Estimate the percentage of your energies you give to each quadrant. Ideally you will be concentrating on the red hot and the hot priorities.

- Think hard about how to reduce time and effort spent in the other two quadrants.

- For each priority, make a note of 2 actions that will take you closer to a result.

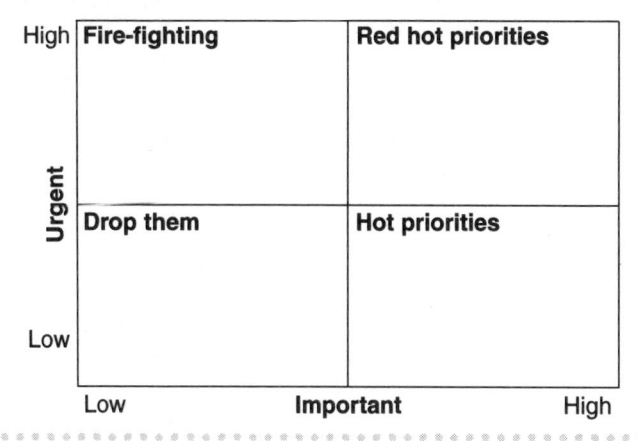

Urgent		
High	**Fire-fighting**	**Red hot priorities**
	Drop them	**Hot priorities**
Low		
	Low —— Important —— High	

Life priorities

Shirley Conran wrote the groundbreaking book *Superwoman* in the 70s. One of the sayings from that book, which changed the way that women thought about their priorities, was, '*Life's too short to stuff a mushroom*'. How would you complete the sentence: Life's too short to............................?

Planning your time well

You have identified your £100 priorities and the actions that are going to have the biggest impact on your objectives. But when you arrive at the end of the day, or the end of the week you find that time has run out before your priorities have. Life can be messy and it can be hard to keep on top of the daily demands. A technique that can help is to make a list: a to-do list, not a wish list.

How to write a to-do list

- Identify all of the activities you think you need to do over the day (or the week). Focus on the important and urgent things, not the routine things.
- Rate them as (A) high (B) medium or (C) low priority, balancing importance and urgency.
- Focus on the As and on how and when you will do them.
- Tick them off as you do them. Don't write lots of quick and easy Cs just so you can see lots of ticks!
- If you find some of the Cs are being carried forward day after day, do you really need to do them?
- If you need to add a new task, rate it too and re-prioritise your list if necessary.

Healthy habits

Now you know *what* you have to do. Next you have to decide *when* you will do it. You need to plan. Here are some hints about planning and scheduling your day.

- Set start and stop times for each activity.
- Set aside specific times for things like making all your telephone calls or dealing with all your mail.
- Make sure you have scheduled in the As on your list first.
- Be realistic. Don't try to plan every minute. That can cause great feelings of pressure.
- Leave time for breaks and for thinking time.

Pick your times carefully for hot priority activities. Plan to do them when you are in peak form. Everyone has their own energy cycle and peaks at different points in the day.

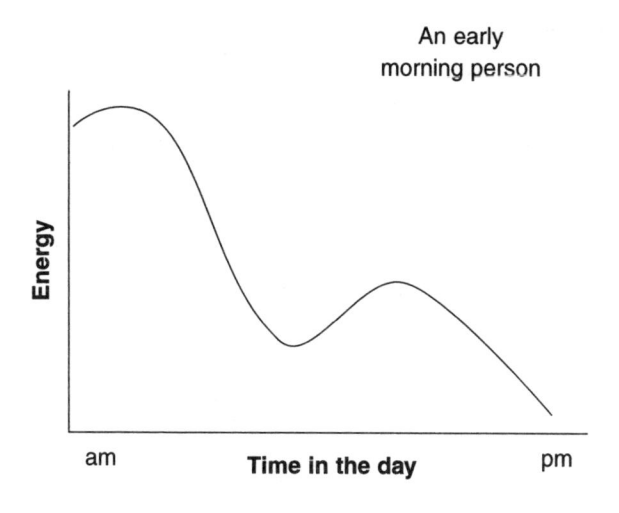

An early morning person

A slow starter

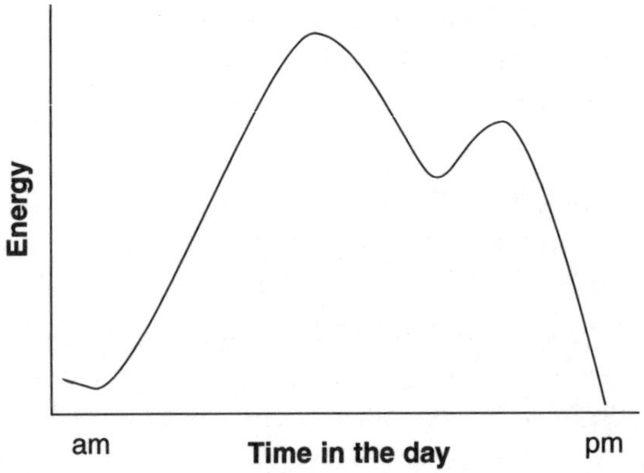

Test yourself

When are you at your best?

Do you leap up in the morning ready to get going? Or are you a slow starter? Do you find you do your best work in the early afternoon when you're fully charged up? Plot your energy cycle.

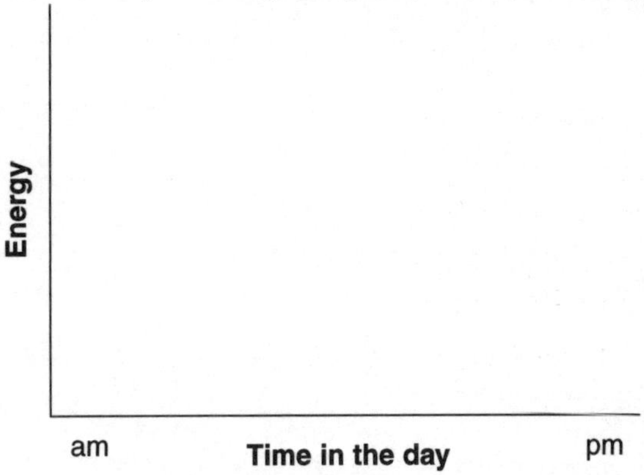

Try to set aside 'prime time' for the important activities at the peak of your energy curve. The worst time to tackle a hot priority is when your energy cycle is at its ebb.

Healthy habits

> *'All the staff infighting and squabbling was causing the President many sleepless afternoons.'* Patrick Buchanan, on the Reagan administration.

Test yourself

How organised are you?

Circle the numbers showing how strongly you agree or disagree with each statement. Ticks on the left always mean 'disagree'. Ticks to the right always mean 'agree'.

	Disagree			Agree
1. I make a daily list of all the things I have to do	1	2	3	4
2. I jump around from one task to another	4	3	2	1
3. I try to avoid taking work home with me	1	2	3	4
4. I do the things I like to do first putting off the other things as long as I can	4	3	2	1
5. I set aside time for planning and thinking about how I'm going to do my work	1	2	3	4
6. I rarely get everything on my to-do list done	4	3	2	1
7. I know my 'prime time' for getting things done and build that into my planning	1	2	3	4
8. My desk is a mess/disorganised	4	3	2	1

9. I prioritise things on my to-do list into categories A, B & C	1	2	3	4
10. Even when I'm busy I find it hard to say 'no' when asked to take on something	4	3	2	1

Total your scores.

Interpretation guidelines

30–40: You manage your time well.

20–29: You have scope for improvement. Examine your low scores and identify how you can reduce your stress by changing the ways you work.

Under 19: You are not managing time well and are making things harder for yourself and possibly for those around you. Look over your scores and focus on one or two key areas. Decide what you will do differently. Persuade others to give you feedback and support in your efforts to change.

Be sure to build *recovery periods* into your stress management planning. These give you something to look forward to when the going gets rough. Without them stress can mount up and be more difficult to manage. You might take a daily walk round the block at lunchtime. Or attend a regular fitness class. Perhaps you might watch your favourite soap when everything stops in your house.

You can stage a recovery period at almost any quiet time by using visualisation – picturing in your imagination something that makes you feel good.

> *Practising visualising*
>
> - Get into a really comfortable position.
> - Think about your breathing: breathe in and out smoothly and slowly.
> - Visualise an event that you are proud of being involved in, or one that was a very happy time for you, or particularly memorable or important. Or visualise someone who is dear to you.
> - Pretend you have a videotape of this event and play it over slowly in your mind's eye.
> - Fast forward it or replay bits you particularly like.
> - Think of the sounds, the sights, the smells at this event.
> - How does this make you feel? Stay with the good times and the feelings.
> - Hold on to those feelings as you come back to the present.
> - Open your eyes; collect your thoughts; come back slowly to the present.

2. Asserting yourself

Do you ever say 'yes' but really mean 'absolutely not'? Do you ever think 'I wish I'd said what I really felt'? Do you ever feel that your needs and rights have just got trampled on again? By not asserting your needs or plans you may leave yourself open to being exploited. Being assertive often helps to avoid stress. You feel better about yourself as well.

Being assertive means

- having respect for your own needs/point of view
- having respect for the needs and viewpoints of the other party
- aiming for an 'I win and you win' outcome
- being open and honest with yourself and with others
- listening to other people's point of view
- being clear about what you want and not being sidetracked

Saying yes earns lots of brownie points. Therefore it can be difficult saying no when you want to. Especially if you have a strong Please Others driver (Chapter 2). Saying 'no' can invite criticism and make you feel guilty. It is however perfectly OK to make your own choices, based on your own priorities. It's OK to say no.

Some tips for saying no and meaning it.

- Really mean it. If you don't, or if your body language is saying 'maybe', you will be pestered until you change your mind.
- If you 're not sure what you want to do, say you'll decide later. Repeat the message like a broken record until the other person gets the point.
- If they raise other objections, say 'I understand you're upset/this may make it difficult for you/you were relying on me but I can't do it/don't want to do it/am saying no.'
- Don't go overboard apologising. You have the right to say no.
- If you have a compromise to offer, propose it. But

> make sure the timing is right. Again stick to the
> message 'I understand that wasn't quite what you
> wanted/I understand that you are upset about this
> but it's all I can do'

Sticking to your guns takes practice. Try out this exercise with a friend so you can feel what it's like to say the words and get your point across clearly and assertively. Think of situations where you wished you'd been more assertive and practise different, more assertive, responses. For example, your boss has asked you to stay late to finish an important document. You've made other arrangements which would be difficult to change. How might you have stuck to your guns? Another example: you want the children to clean up their room/pick up their clothes/keep the stereo volume lower. And another: you want to make an appointment to see your boss. She is always in a hurry and never has her diary with her. You have been trying for quite some time to get this arranged. You want to get her to agree to a specific time. Play out in your mind how you would handle these situations assertively.

3. Looking after yourself

If you hear a funny knocking in the engine of your car, you are unlikely to keep going and ignore it. You would certainly have it checked out before it becomes a serious problem. Similarly you fill up with the right fuel, check the oil level regularly, and ensure that the engine is getting what it needs to run properly.

You may be looking after your car better than you look after yourself. Do you remember when things are hectic at work and your back was playing up again? Did you get it checked out? Did you watch your posture and do something about your fitness level? Is your life is so busy that you seem to live on takeaways, quick fry ups, and alcohol 'to help you relax'?

People often ignore their health as long as they can still cope. But looking after yourself is important for handling stress successfully. Follow these simple guidelines:

Diet
Eat a balanced diet which includes fresh fruit and vegetables. Keep alcohol consumption to safe levels. Avoid tobacco and recreational drugs. Avoid fad diets which have you eating nothing but bananas or cabbage for days on end. Your aim should be to find a healthy eating pattern which you can stick to, and which you enjoy. Make sure you include some treats in it. Being too rigid about diet can be another source of stress.

Eat regularly – preferably little and often. Skipping meals makes your energy level dip. You may then want a boost with caffeine or an instant energy rush from sweet food or chocolate. If you keep dealing with your energy 'lows' in this way you'll find that your energy level will swing up and down, and your mood may go up and down with it.

Exercise your body
Try to build some regular exercise into your daily routine. Walking costs nothing, needs no special equipment and can be done at any time. Walk to work. Walk up stairs rather than take the lift. Try yoga or belly-dancing or gentle jogging. Adopt the 'use it or lose it' principle and make sure that you do use as many muscles as possible. Bend and stretch. Play catch with your children. Chase kites on windy days.

Healthy habits

Exercise your mind
Don't be a mental couch potato. Keep your mind as active as your body so that both are 'fit enough to handle stress.' A good book can be a real relaxer for many. Do (or try) the crossword every day in the newspaper. Keep a diary. Become a member of the Trivial Pursuit team at your local. Use it or lose it applies to the mind as well as the body.

Switch off
Take time to relax and enjoy yourself. For some people it can be a hobby, a love of music, a regular Sunday friendly soccer match followed by Sunday lunch in the pub, a regular appointment for a back and shoulder massage. Look for ways to switch off that work for you and fit with your lifestyle.

Stability zones
It is important to have stable elements in your life. Like those wobbly dolls with weighted bases, stability zones help you bounce back and regain your balance after being knocked by stressful events. Stability zones can be places, objects, people, organisations, hobbies or values. Anything that makes you feel good – especially when it seems that everything is against you.

Test yourself

Find the stable zones in your life

What are the places where you feel at home, or you feel you belong?
What are your favourite objects which can make you feel good just looking at them because of the memories they bring?
Who are the people you rely on?
What organisations do you belong to which are important to you?

- What are your hobbies, the things that take your mind off things?
- What are the beliefs and values that provide that basis for your day-to-day living?

4. Maintaining relationships and networks

Last, though certainly not least, are your relationships and networks. Social support networks typically include friends, family, and work colleagues. Not only do people in your network provide practical help when you are under pressure, they may also help you see things differently. Relationships and networks are mutual affairs. At times you will be giver, and at others the receiver of support. It is an interesting fact that being supportive of others is its own reward. It can make you feel better and happier.

What a support network offers:

- Practical help – the friend who will babysit in an emergency
- Mutual support – a sense of give and take
- Acceptance – being loved or needed or being important to someone else
- Emotional support – especially when you feel that things are going against you
- A reality check – they know you and can tell when you indulge in 'stinking thinking' or have lost the plot, and they can help you find it again.

Social support is not about how many people you are acquainted with. It is more about quality than quantity.

Healthy habits

What is important is having one or two people you feel close to and can rely on – having a shoulder to cry on sometimes; having someone tell you you look good in the new sweater; having a work colleague sharing the same pressures.

Now may be the time to establish new relationships or renew neglected friendships. In the 60s and 70s dancing was one of the social pastimes where many people made friends and met future partners. Church was another popular meeting place. Nowadays it's more difficult to think of equivalent meeting grounds. Perhaps it is most difficult of all for older people. Moreover, because of work demands and other pressures, important relationships may not have received the attention they deserve.

Re-building your social network may require initiative. You might suggest going out for a meal, meeting for a Saturday morning coffee or going to see that new blockbuster film. You may want to think if there are any ways in which you could offer support to a family member, friend or colleague who is under pressure.

One good way to extend your networks might be to identify where you can meet people with the same interests or hobbies. If you have always had a yen to tap dance or throw pots this could be the time to do that, and at the same time to meet new people with kindred spirits.

Your local gym may be your favourite stress-busting resource. It may also run social events patronised by fellow fitness fans. Our local sports centre, where one of the authors had a regular swim, was in fact running a dance. You might imagine her reaction when greeted by another early swimmer with the words 'I didn't recognise you with your clothes on!'

For some people, pets can be an important non-human part of their support network. A pet can offer unconditional affection. It can be a source of enjoyment, a companion and an indirect aid in keeping healthy.

- Who makes up your social support network?
- Have you let some important relationships slip?
- Do you need to do any work on them?
- Do you need to do some relationship maintenance work?

Chapter review: what you will do differently

What thoughts will you take from this chapter? What ideas will you apply? What will you do differently?

- Managing time and setting priorities

- Asserting myself

- Looking after myself

- Managing relationships and support networks

Stress at work

We noted in Chapter 1 the damaging impact of stress on individuals in organisations, and on the ability of organisations to achieve their goals because of stress. No kind of organisation is exempt – schools, businesses, local authorities, government offices, voluntary organisations and institutes. All are affected and there is much to be done to make them better places to be.

> *The Times* of December 5, 2000 reported that
>
> '*A teacher who was forced to retire early after two breakdowns has been awarded ... £254,362 for the "intolerable" working conditions at the school.*' Her union said they were dealing at any one time with 120 stress-related compensation claims.

Everyone has a part to play in this endeavour, particularly managers, supervisors, trade unions and other opinion leaders. Managing stress effectively means removing the conditions that cause it in the first place, and, where that is not possible, providing the means for recovery and the restoration of balance and well-being.

In the chapter we describe how to manage stress at work within a logical framework:

- Acknowledging that stress is a problem
- Auditing stress and its causes
- Designing improvement solutions
- Implementing them
- Monitoring and evaluating those measures.

The chapter concludes with some final thoughts on the kind of organisation that is stress-resistant.

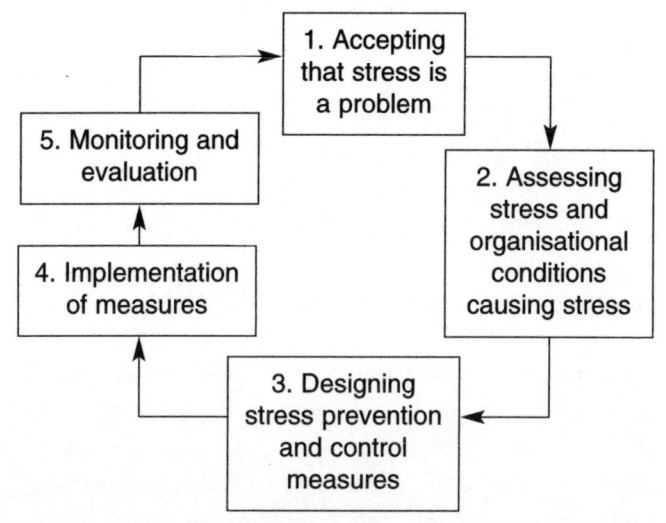

Stress-management model

1. Accepting there is a problem

Organisations as well as individuals are prone to the boiled frog syndrome. Everyone in a group might be feeling stressed, but no one wants to admit it. For there is often a stigma associated with being stressed. It may be perceived as a weakness. Macho culture is another reason – 'If you can't stand the heat get out of the kitchen'. But as we have discussed, everyone is potentially subject to stress, even the most robust.

> Chairman Lee Iacocca was hired to turn around the ailing Chrysler Corporation. He described his reactions to this enormous challenge: 'I was scared inside ...

> that the total would collapse or that I'd collapse physically. And I got nervous. At one time I went into the Surgeon-General's office. I was sort of seeing double. It had suddenly hit me ... at the Congressional hearings (on the loan guarantee). There were weeks and weeks of boning up and answering questions and I got addle-brained. I really began to get fuzzy. That's the only time I worried about myself.' (Nicholson, 1981)

Managing stress starts with acceptance that stress is a problem for you, for others and for the organisation. Organisations are under ever-increasing pressure for higher performance, improved safety, greater responsiveness to customers' and public demands, newer and better products and services, and lower costs. Schools face pressures from educational reforms, teacher shortages and violence from pupils. Political coercion and public expectations to reduce waiting lists cause intense pressure in the NHS. And as the pressures rise so too does stress and the incidence of burnout.

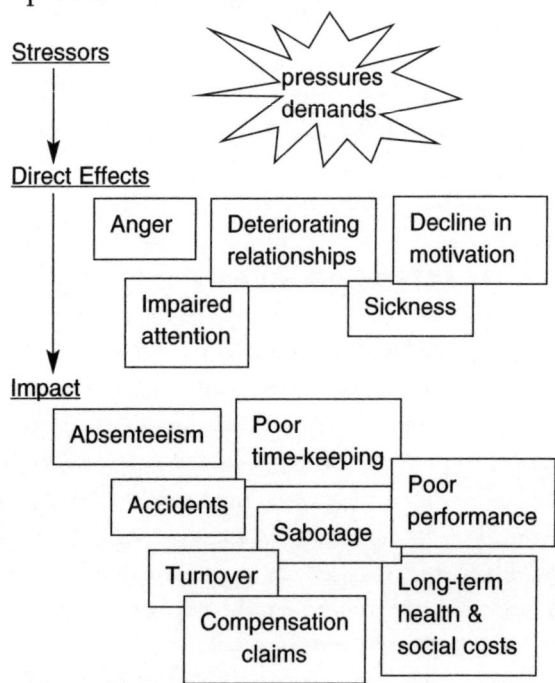

The symptoms and effects are there or all to see:

Stressors → pressures, demands

Direct Effects: Anger, Deteriorating relationships, Decline in motivation, Impaired attention, Sickness

Impact: Absenteeism, Poor time-keeping, Accidents, Poor performance, Sabotage, Turnover, Compensation claims, Long-term health & social costs

2. Stress assessment

While there may be a will to manage it effectively, the scope and causes of organisational stress may not be clear. The extent of organisational stress and the conditions that are causing it can be observed and assessed by:

- monitoring vital organisational statistics and trends
- listening to people – sounds simple, doesn't it
- carrying out questionnaire-based surveys.

Vital statistics
Rises in these six objective statistics are frequent signs of organisational stress. It pays to monitor them regularly.

- lateness rate – often a sign of underlying morale problems
- sickness and other absences
- employee turnover
- accident rate and severity
- grievances filed
- decline in cost/profit performance of individual work units.

As we noted in an earlier case, absenteeism may represent attempts to cope as well as reactions to stress. Being off work gives time out to restore balance. Recognising the value of this, some companies have introduced 'duvet days'. When it all gets too much employees may stay at home, whether or not they stay under the duvet. A duvet day does not count as a sick day or part of regular leave.

Listening to people
Management by walking about (MBWA) is essential for monitoring morale and signs of stress. Get out of the office and into the work place. Pay attention to people *at all levels*. Be open, ask questions and listen. Make it easy for people to talk to you. Tell-tale signs to watch for:

- conflicts and tensions between individuals and between work units
- frustration with management
- cynicism and detachment
- complaints about being under-resourced and overworked
- frustration and emotional storming
- increased use of alcohol.

What may get in the way of listening is a difference in perspective between management and unions. Management tend to focus on individual causes and unions on organisational causes. This difference has a significant impact on the selection and funding of stress interventions. The truth, of course, is that individual factors, organisational conditions and a combination of the two bring about stress.

Questionnaire-based surveys

A stress audit team should, therefore, have among its members an occupational health practitioner and an occupational psychologist. This will make the survey more objective, comprehensive and reliable.

> *Only 8 percent of respondents indicated that a stress audit had been carried out in their organisation in the last year.*
>
> Ruth Wheatley in *'Taking the Strain'*, 2000.

Stress questionnaires for an organisational audit can be purchased off-the-shelf or designed to suit the organisation. The former is probably least expensive and may provide comparisons with other organisations. The latter, however, can be focused at specific areas of greatest interest. The questionnaire will include statements to be rated much as in the following example.

Test yourself

Mini audit

These items are typical of those found in organisational surveys.

Stress at work

	Never stressful			Always stressful	
1. I am not really clear about what is expected of me in my job	1	2	3	4	5
2. I am under continual pressure to keep to tight schedules	1	2	3	4	5
3. The open-plan workplace makes it difficult to concentrate	1	2	3	4	5
4. My work is repetitive and extremely boring	1	2	3	4	5
5. Everyone is quick to blame others when something goes wrong	1	2	3	4	5
6. There is little career opportunity for me here	1	2	3	4	5
7. The general organisational climate is quite unfriendly	1	2	3	4	5
8. Minor decisions are generally made at too high a level	1	2	3	4	5

Normally a stress questionnaire will be completed by a sizeable sample or by everyone in an organisation. The average scores for the group give a good indication of the causes of stress in the various areas of the organisation.

Organisational stress questionnaires typically cover these pressure points and demands that cause stress in organisational life:

1. The job
- too many roles to perform
- ambiguous roles
- job demands – e.g. routine, boring, or very complex
- conflict between roles – e.g. be caring but hit targets

2. Work
- working across organisation boundaries
- customer contact work – e.g. bus driver
- shift work
- no discretion or control

3. Organisation context
- hierarchical structure
- lack of training
- culture
- difficult personalities
- office politics
- bullying

4. Physical environment
- space and place
- technology – inadequate or new
- threats to health – e.g. fire service, armed robbery
- physical conditions

5. Quality of leadership
- dominance
- lack of clarity
- none or poor feedback
- absence of recognition

6. Organisational change
- insufficient information
- unclear direction
- job insecurity
- lack of consultation

An important caveat. Carry out a stress audit only if you are fully prepared to implement measures that people will see as making a difference. If you carry out an audit and do nothing it raises then dashes people's hopes for a better working life. It will make any future attempts to mobilise them that much more difficult.

> 20% of managers experience significant computer anxiety: twice as many women as men.

3. Designing stress prevention and control measures

Once the most significant causes of stress have been identified the next task is to design relevant solutions. Measures for preventing, removing and controlling stress are limited only by the imagination and will of decision makers. Under the following headings think of just one idea for dealing with each stressor in our mini-audit.

1. Lack of job clarity

2. Pressure to keep to tight schedules

3. Open-plan workplace

4. Repetitive and boring work

5. A 'blame culture'

6. Lack of career opportunity

7. Unfriendly organisational climate

8. Over-centralised decision-making

Applied research gives very clear evidence that the following measures reduce stress and improve morale and work satisfaction.

Reduce job pressures
- Treat people as individuals. Remember that everyone has their own stress curve. An exciting challenge for some may be stress-causing for others.
- Match individuals to the jobs they do best. Give greater responsibility, increasing scope and variety of tasks to those who are ready to be stretched.
- Communicate and consult with people about job expectations. Make sure everyone is clear about their responsibilities and targets.
- Enable them to understand how important their job is to the business objectives. Give information on how everyone fits in.
- Ensure that everyone is properly inducted into the organisation and into their job. Provide job training for all who need it.
- Offer regular supervision and support with target setting and feedback.
- Try to give advance notice of urgent or important jobs. Prioritise tasks and cut out unnecessary work.

During the 1980s British Airways was transformed from being an unwieldy, nationalised bureaucracy into a customer-focused business. An important part of the strategy was the active recruitment of front-line staff who actually enjoyed being of service and caring for people.

Reduce work pressures
- Give groups of workers greater responsibility for the effective performance of the group.
- Change the way jobs are done by moving people between jobs.
- Where conflicts exist between home and work, see if there is scope for flexible work schedules. Encourage a flexible approach to managing workload.
- Provide proper resources – time, tools, equipment and back-up geared to the needs of the staff and the task.
- Give people the authority they require to sort out problems to the best of their ability.

Reduce organisational pressures
- Keep people informed about changes that may affect their job, job security and ways of work.
- Design organisational structures to reduce role overlap and conflict.
- Flatten unnecessary hierarchical structures.
- Encourage and support team building and team working.
- Train supervisors and managers in appropriate leadership styles.
- Build trust and respect between managers and staff.
- Provide training on interpersonal skills and conflict management skills.
- Introduce a performance review and appraisal system.
- Introduce a 360 feedback system.
- Introduce effective harassment policies.

- Introduce an agreed grievance procedure and proper investigation of complaints.
- Encourage a culture of openness and transparency.
- Develop a learning culture. Encourage individual development.

Reduce physical pressures

- In some ways these are the easiest to deal with because there is legislation about environmental conditions.
- Ensure that everyone knows and meets their statutory obligations.
- Involve staff in the design of their workplace.
- Provide everyone with training in health and safety.

In selecting, conceiving and planning measures for managing stress, consult and involve as many people as possible. That is, managers and staff at all levels. This will give a wider sense of control and ownership. It will also increase commitment to the new measures. Ideally the measures will be planned and supported by both management and unions.

4. Implementation of prevention and control

The caveats and suggestions mooted above apply very much to implementation:

- Don't initiate stress management unless prepared to follow through to completion.
- Have a united approach by management and labour.
- Consult and involve, don't impose stress-management measures.

There are further commonsense steps to consider:

- *Plan* the implementation of the stress management strategy. Resource it adequately as you would any other important business initiative.
- Beware of overloading people with lots of new stress-management projects. Phase them in.
- Go for quick wins that make an obvious difference.
- Be sure that people appreciate the advantages of the new measures.
- Beware of branding and publicising the new measures as 'special programmes'. Better to introduce them naturally into the fabric of organisational life.

5. Monitoring and evaluation

To successfully prevent and manage workplace stress the organisation needs to ensure that the new measures are doing the business. The stress temperature needs to be monitored regularly. This means ongoing collection and analysis of key statistics. It means continuing management-by-walking-about. And it means repeated administrations of the stress audit – perhaps at annual intervals. Managers and unions, together, must keep their fingers on the organisational pulse. They must be on the alert for the warning signs.

6. Organisation development: final thoughts

Clearly the most effective measures are the ones that prevent stress from happening in the first place.

> *'The best armour is to keep out of range.'*
>
> Italian proverb

This may mean taking a close look at the whole organisation – and perhaps re-inventing it. If that seems to be a promising direction, you might like to find out more about 'organisational development' (OD). Informed sources can be found in the ranks of organisational psychologists, management consultants and human resources specialists.

In our own OD research we have found that healthy, productive organisations share a number of characteristics, and the underlying theme is how these organisations deal with change.

```
1 Open dynamic culture
2 Inspiring direction
3 People-oriented leadership
4 Positive power relationships
        ↓
  Healthy organisation
        ↓
Wide commitment
Goal achievement
Individual satisfaction & effectiveness
```

1. An open, dynamic culture

This means creating a lively environment where people can raise difficult issues without fear. Where it is safe to raise one's head above the parapet. Where people are encouraged to take sensible risks and make decisions. It means having resources to support and encourage new ideas and better ways of doing things. A change-supporting environment is not handicapped with excessive bureaucracy that gets in the way of action and slows down decisions. It provides time, training and whatever other resources are needed by those who have been tasked with making change happen.

2. A positive, inspiring direction

People, and businesses, prosper when they have clear, challenging and relevant goals to guide their actions. By relevant we mean goals that are in keeping with the organisation's capacities and with the market's demands. Clarity of direction is particularly difficult, and particularly important, when steering change. It is also important to build a consensus and support for the direction among the organisation's members. Clarity and consensus aren't easily achieved, and once achieved may need to be re-established and renewed after periods of turbulence. Sound planning, organisation of resources and control of the action taken are all critical if the direction is to be successfully implemented. Guiding the direction of change, finally, requires a finely judged balance between staying the course over the longer term, changing it as the unforeseen future unfolds, and exploiting emerging opportunities.

3. People-Oriented Leadership

When we talk about leaders, we do not only mean those at the top. We mean people at all levels who influence things. Giving positive leadership means being attentive to and unselfishly serving others. This is usually difficult in times of change when managers' and team leaders' tasks increase exponentially, and when they themselves feel overworked and under-appreciated. Yet this is the time when leadership comes into its own. People will go the extra mile and share the extra burden if there is someone in their corner, if they know what to expect in the broader sense and in the sense of how they must perform, if they enjoy the trust of their manager or if they have been involved in the change process. Leaders inform, they respond to people's need to understand, and they teach people how to handle change effectively.

4. Relationships and Power

Maintaining good relationships and exercising power responsibly is a challenge and a condition of organisational change. Effective masters of change develop networks and coalitions that enable them to get things done. Their self-interest is both enlightened and aligned with the corporate interest. They aim to have constructive relationships with their bosses and colleagues. They understand and resist the temptations of power politics and erosive internecine conflict. They understand and use their personal and position power wisely. People are expected and encouraged to work together across boundaries, to seek win-win solutions and to serve their internal customers well.

In conclusion, the single most significant contribution to improving the situation in organisations is this: to think less about managing stress and more about making the organisation a healthier and happier place to be.

Chapter review

- What ideas will you take away from this chapter?
- With whom will you discuss these ideas?
- Which will you put into practice?

Being resilient

Like others who write on the subject, our thoughts to this point have largely been about understanding and 'fixing' stress. As we have shown, this is important and much can be done to handle stress successfully. In this concluding chapter we shift focus from 'fixing' stress to being well. Being well and being whole is everyone's goal and lies at the root of self-esteem.

> "Self-esteem is how you feel when you are striving wholeheartedly for worthwhile things; it's how you experience yourself when you are using your abilities to the fullest in the service of what you deeply value. It's not about displaying your traits advantageously or showing that yours are better than someone else's. . . what feeds your self-esteem – meeting challenges with high effort and using your abilities to help others – is also what makes for a productive and constructive life."
> Professor Carol Dweck, psychologist

Imagine you have a magic wand and, with a touch of the wand, you find yourself in a world where you are wholly fulfilled. Your life has meaning, it makes sense. You are quietly confident and feel good about yourself. You are connected to others. There is much in your life that you can influence, and what you can't influence you accept. You feel in control of your fate and are willing to take sensible risks. You are able to bounce back from the troubles that life brings. Got the picture?

> ## ❓ Test Yourself
>
> **Applying the magic wand**
>
> If you felt wholly fulfilled, complete and 'together'
> - What would be different in your life?
> - What would be different about your relationships?
> - What would you be doing more?
> - What would you stop doing or be doing less?

Of course you have no magic wand any more than we know the secrets of wellbeing and wholeness. The transition to being the most that you can be is perhaps best conceived as a journey. And for the journey it is important to have a some guidelines and landmarks to steer by. There are four that we find most useful:

- stay in touch with yourself
- make positive choices
- think beyond yourself
- stretch yourself

1. Stay in touch with yourself

The first guideline is to know and understand yourself and accept who you are. For this part of the journey an openness of spirit, a continuing willingness to learn about yourself is essential. There are definite and positive steps you can take to stay in touch with yourself.

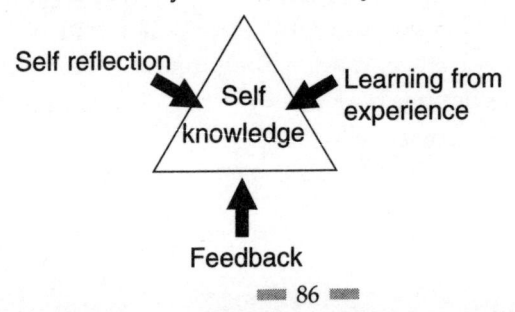

Self reflection → Self knowledge ← Learning from experience ↑ Feedback

Being resilient

Self reflection
Everyone has a capacity for self-reflection – for looking inwards, examining and being aware of every aspect of themselves – memories of growing up, feelings about people we meet and the situations we encounter, what we intend to do next week, and so forth. However, the capacity for looking inwards usually requires practice, especially for those who are strongly action-oriented and not naturally inclined towards reflection. So consider how and when you will practice introspecting. Psychological questionnaires about interests, preference, motives and personality are a good jumping off point for exploring the self.

Learning from experience
People can also learn about themselves through their daily experiences, problems and the relationships they engage in. Our book *Test Your Potential* says more about learning from experience. We all learn from experience and there are practical ways to do this effectively.

Feedback
Another positive measure is to be open to feedback from others who know you. A structured process, 360 degree feedback which has been introduced into organisational life, shows much promise for improving self-awareness and self-development. You can achieve the same benefit informally by asking a few friends and colleagues the following simple questions.

> To be as effective as I can be:
> - what might I do more of?
> - what might I do less of?
> - what might I continue to do?

Now ask yourself: what gets in the way of me staying in touch with myself? In fact, we all have similar hang ups. One obstacle is that most of us are quite sensitive, we want to hear what people think of us but we also fear it will be critical. Clearly, the climate and the setting need to be right for receiving feedback. So think about how to set the scene before asking for feedback.

> Tips for receiving feedback
> - Firstly, acknowledge that you will almost certainly hear feedback you won't like. That is normal, but such feedback will help you improve. Think of the missed opportunity for self-improvement – if no one told you about your body odour!
> - Explain the purpose – which is to help you understand yourself better. Before you meet, give the person time to think of what their feed back will be.
> - Arrange a quiet time and comfortable setting to have your discussion.
> - Make it easy for the other person to share what they have experienced in their dealings with you. Listen actively. Do not challenge, disagree or 'yes, but'. If you need more understanding ask if they can give you examples, or if they can explain the point more fully.
> - Pay as much attention to the 'good stuff' as the criticism. Do not discount it or dismiss it, show that it pleases you.
> - At the conclusion thank the person, whatever the nature of their feedback.

Another common obstacle to self-understanding is not wanting to fall short of our internal standards – conscious or otherwise. Because comparisons of this sort may give rise to unpleasant feelings, we sometimes block out perceived shortcomings in self-defense. This is why some people are quite blind to imperfections that are evident to everyone else.

Furthermore, to escape damaging self-knowledge, people sometimes resort to alcohol and drug abuse which reduces self-awareness and self-inhibition. The self-dislike that self-awareness brings may also lead to bulimia or anorexia.

Wellbeing and wholeness mean accepting that you are not perfect. No one is. Being whole means consciously accepting your life history, with its failures and successes, looking forward and moving on. Accepting that you are who you are doesn't mean you stop developing or cease to strive. Self-acceptance is the starting point for becoming what you can and want to be.

2. Make positive choices

We have found that wellbeing is closely linked to adopting a positive attitude towards life and change, not an unrealistic attitude, but one that is uncompromisingly positive. Positive people acknowledge their misfortunes and those which others experience. They grieve over their losses and are saddened by the tribulations and losses of others. What they avoid doing is dwelling on their troubles or the troubles of the world. They may disagree, take issue, and oppose, but we don't hear them ranting on or endlessly complaining.

We can think of no better role model than Nelson Mandela who, throughout his long years as a political prisoner, continued to oppose apartheid, refusing to compromise his principles. Neither during his imprisonment nor when liberated, did Mandela complain about the personal suffering he endured. Without his living example of fortitude, it is inconceivable that the supporters of institutionalised state oppression would have been won over.

Living positively means retaining and exercising the will to make positive choices, even in the most hostile of circumstances. Victor Frankl, the noted psychiatrist, observed this while a prisoner in the Nazi concentration camps of World War II. In spite of the profound deprivation and despotism they endured, certain Jewish prisoners retained an extraordinary sense of control in the most ordinary of circumstances. They exercised choice by subdividing their meagre bread rations and holding back a portion, uneaten. The portion they saved they chose to give it to those in greatest need who suffered most.

In more modern times, a tale with a moral is told by Dr Spencer Johnson in his little book, *Who Moved My Cheese?* The heroes of the tale are two mice, who one day discover that their regular and seemingly infinite supply of cheese has dwindled to nothing. Accepting this new reality, the two unlikely heroes make difficult yet positive choices. The story goes on to describe their trials, openness, determination and learning as they successfully adapt to radical change. Contrasting with their positive behaviour is the self-defeating conduct of their two contemporaries – who refuse to accept change, live in the past and fail to make choices. It is definitely well worth a read.

Those who have a positive mind-set have a knack of seeing silver linings where others see only clouds, they have skills at turning problems into opportunities. It is a bit like putting a painting in just the right frame to bring out its unique beauty. By placing a situation in the right frame the possibilities and advantages are highlighted. Suppose, for instance, that a colleague gives you feedback that is true but critical. You might see this in a frame of failure or a frame of disloyalty or, as this quote illustrates, in a frame of self-improvement.

> 'The top performers ask a further question: 'What do I need to learn?' They don't waste time berating themselves for doing something badly. They look for shortfalls that impede their use of strengths, and for corrections. . . From 'What do I need to learn?' comes a variety of follow-ups. 'What am I doing that I should do more of? That I should cut down? In what areas do I need to improve? What is the most effective way to get up to speed? Or can I delegate any of these areas to someone else?'
>
> (Garfield, 1986)

3. Think beyond yourself

The senses of self and self-esteem develop within the web of relationships each of us has – with family, friends, work associates, acquaintances and with the larger community. The temptation is to take people and relationships for granted, in fact, they need constant nurturing and attention and going beyond a pre-occupation with self.

Going beyond the absorption each one of us has with oneself is a recurring theme in the self-development literature. This is known as self-transcendence and it means being interested in and concerned about bigger, collective issues. Once again Nelson Mandela is our role model *par excellence*. Below are his words, spoken in court when facing the death penalty at the age of 46:

> 'During my lifetime I have dedicated my life to this struggle of the African people. I have fought against white domination, and I have fought against black domination. I have cherished the ideals of a democratic and free society in which all persons live together in harmony with equal opportunities. It is an ideal I hope to live for, and to see realized. But, My Lord, if needs be it is an ideal for which I am prepared to die.'
>
> (Nelson Mandela, 1964)

It is this wider concern that motivates some to take up lives of service and experienced people to want to give something back, this is considered to be characteristic of those who have an advanced stage of personality development. Carl Jung, one of the most famous psychologists and contributors of the 20th century, writes about no longer being 'that touchy, egotistical bundle of personal wishes, fears, hopes and ambitions' and moving instead into 'absolute, binding, and indissoluble communion with the world at large. The complications arising at this stage are no longer egotistic wish-conflicts, but difficulties that concern others as much as oneself.' (1954)

It is not just Nobel Prize winners who achieve this level of development.

> Marianne and Joe are a middle-aged couple. They live comfortably and their two children are grown up and doing well for themselves. As she is deeply concerned about the well-being of children, Marianne works as a volunteer telephone counsellor for a children's charity while both believe that education plays a vital part in the development of a decent society. Joe serves as an active school governor at the local school.

4. Stretch yourself

As we noted earlier (page 14), absence of pressure does not bring contentment. Striving and being stretched are healthy and necessary for wellbeing and self-improvement. So the fourth guideline is to keep reaching beyond yourself, to keep extending your potential.

> An amateur runner in his free time, Tony realises that 'you never go faster if you don't do anything different'. So in training he will keep at his regular pace for a mile, step it up for a minute, revert to jogging for another mile, then another burst of speed, and so on. By practicing fartlek running, Tony has steadily raised his performance and his standing in competitive runs.

Stretching means stepping outside the comfort zone, going beyond the point where pressure is comfortable. To ensure that your personal resources are up to the pressure, there is a continuing need to check how you feel – to test your resilience. Take regular soundings about how you are feeling and how you are coping any time you approach or exceed the bad-stress limit on the Stress Curve, when you observe the pressure approaching the stress level you ease up and step back to the comfort zone. Stepping back allows time for reflection, consolidating the learning, and restoring your resources for the next stretch.

Practice and repetition are key elements of resilience, what at first is clumsy and feels unnatural becomes skilled and second nature with practice. Top sports performers and athletes use the expression 'muscle memory' to describe this result of repetitive practice. And, of course, the same principle applies to personal and interpersonal learning. Stretching,

The stress curve

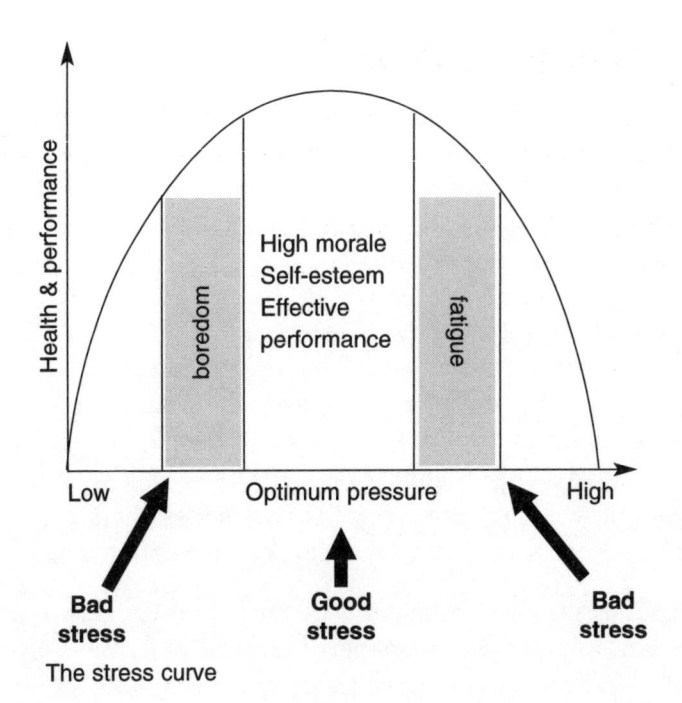

[Chart showing health & performance vs pressure, with regions labeled: boredom, High morale / Self-esteem / Effective performance, fatigue. Arrows indicate Bad stress (low), Good stress (optimum), Bad stress (high).]

pushing the limits, easing up, reflecting and practicing lead to self-development, wellbeing and wholeness.

Conclusion

There are therefore two facets to stress. One is about preventing it and fixing it through understanding and good stress-management practice, and the other is about strengthening your resilience by extending and developing yourself. Both are important for a constructive and productive life. Make it happen.

Chapter review

What thoughts will you take away from this chapter?

Sources and references

Alder, B. *Motivation, Emotion and Stress*, BPS Books, 1999.

Bartlett, D. *Stress, perspectives and processes*, Open University Press, 1998.

Bachen, E., Cohen, S., Marsland, A.L. *Psychoimmunology*, in A. Baum, S. Newman, J. Weinman, R. West, & C. McManus (Eds) *Cambridge Handbook of Psychology, Health and Medicine*, Cambridge University Press, 1997.

Case Report: Stress in the Workplace, from Encyclopaedia of Employment Law and Practice Issue 7 November 2000, Gee Publishing.

Crombie, I.K. *A Pocket Guide to Critical Appraisal*, BMA, 1996.

Dickson, A. *A Woman in Your Own Right*, Quartet Books, 1982.

Dweck, C.S. *Self-Theories.* Psychology Press, 2000.

Evans, P.D. & Edgerton, N. *Life events and mood as predictors of the common cold, British Journal of Medical Psychology*, 64, 35–44.

Fontana, D. *Managing Time*, BPS Books, 1993.

Fennell, M.J.V. *Overcoming Low Self-Esteem*, Robinson, 1999.

Gallwey, T. *The Inner Game of Tennis*, Macmillan, 1986.

Health and Safety Executive. *Stress at Work. A Guide for Employers.*

Hygge, S. *Noise: effects on health,* in A. Baum, S. Newman, J. Weinman, R. West, & C. McManus (Eds) Cambridge Handbook of Psychology, Health and Medicine. Cambridge: Cambridge Universtiy Press, 1997.

Johnson, S. *Who Moved My Cheese*, Random House, 1998.

Kobasa, S.C., Maddi, S.R., & Kahn, S. *Hardiness and Health: a prospective study*, in *Journal of Personality and Social Psychology*, 42, 168–177.

Lazarus, R.S. *Stress and Emotion, a new synthesis*, Free Asociation Books, 1999.

Levy, S., & Heiden, L. *Depression, distress and immunity: risk factors for infectious diseases*, in *Stress Medicine*, 7, 45–51.

Michelli, D. *Successful Assertiveness in a Week*, Hodder & Stoughton, 1994.

Miller, M.A., & Rahe, R.H. *Life changes scaling for the 1990s*, in *Journal of Psychosomatic Research*, 43, 279–292.

Mruk, C.J. *Self-Esteem: Research, Theory and Practice*, Free Association Books, 1999.

O'Neill, B. & O'Neill, L. *Test Your Potential*, Hodder & Stoughton, 2000.

Quick, J.C., & Quick, J.D. *Organizational Stress and Preventive Management*, McGraw-Hill, 1984.

Roger, D. & Nash, P. The Work Skills Centre, Department of Psychology, University of York, Heslington, York YO1 5DD.

Ross, R.S., & Altmaier, E.M. *Intervention in Occupational Stress*, Sage, 1994.

Stewart, I., Joines, V. *TA Today: A New Introduction to Transactional Analysis*, Life space Publishing, 1987.

Sutherland, V.J., & Cooper, C.L. *Understanding Stress*, Chapman & Hall, 1990.

The Scale of Occupational Stress: the Bristol Stress and Health Study, Health and Safety Executive, May 2000.

Wheatley, R. *Taking the Strain*, Institute of Management, 2000.

Zuckerman, M., Eysenck, S., & Eysenck, H.J. *Sensation seeking in England and America: cross cultural age, and sex comparisons, Journal of Clinical and Consulting Psychology*, 46, 139–149.